Nowhere Near As Safe As A Snake In Bed

Susie Wilson

VERVE
POETRY PRESS
BIRMINGHAM

PUBLISHED BY VERVE POETRY PRESS
https://vervepoetrypress.com
mail@vervepoetrypress.com

All rights reserved
© 2024 Susie Wilson

The right of Susie Wilson to be identified as author of this work has been asserted in accordance with section 77 of the Copyright, Designs and Patents Act 1988.

No part of this work may be reproduced, stored or transmitted in any form or by any means, graphic, electronic, recorded or mechanical, without the prior written permission of the publisher.

FIRST PUBLISHED NOV 2024

Printed and bound in the UK
by Imprint Digital, Exeter

ISBN: 978-1-913917-64-7

*To Mack, Max and Jack,
who live it with me.*

CONTENTS

Summer of '76	5
What would you do?	6
Wee Sleakit Cowrin' Beastie	8
Change into this please	9
Banana Circus	10
What they don't tell you about surgery	11
Drains	12
Mr Rex and I	14
Wild Type	15
Hot Woman	17
Mrs Sisyphus	19
sharks don't get cancer.	20
Hope is a Thing with Cells	22
The Coffin Road	24
On cutting my hair before Stereotactic Radiosurgery on my brain	25
The Truth About Hats	27
Charm	28

Acknowledgements

Summer of '76

sun

baby

What would you do?

The gene therapy consultant is breathtaking in her beauty. She
emerges from her room to greet new patients, in orange.
She seems almost all orange, drawing you towards her sweet
bright fruit, down a clean white tunnel corridor.

You alight on a chair, temporarily stunned
by this segment of promising health, so confident,
demonstrating itself. Pre pandemic plastic gowns and masks,
nothing rustles except for her skirt. You are aroused,
but probably by fear, however kindly she says: 'Hello, Susan.'

What you hear next is, 'I am Doctor Arbor' - you've been teaching
Ovid's Latin, so you expect a tree - but the contexts of this
meeting are all wrong. She is not a shrub
from 2,000 years ago. She won't suddenly become,
mid-consult, a river, or a constellation you can use to navigate.

Nor is she a feeding bowl in a zoo pavilion, built to show
and contain Papilionoidea. She is a medical expert softening
her exterior, before commencing complex explanations of how her
special interest - *adjuvant gene therapy* - may buy you time,
to stop the melanomas grubbing inside your shins.

It is their lifecycle we want to turn off. Prevent
their genes doing a new job on you. Halt militant proteins,
determined to hatch once warm, then caterpillar along, eating
their way out of your lungs, breasts, bone or brain.

Stopping the monster from splitting to shed its skin
even once would be a triumph, as far as you are concerned.
No more pupae. Please. And while the beautiful doctor talks,
clouds of probabilities flutter around her office,

butterflies circling your heads in swift loops of likelihoods,
which you hardly understand. Then one fact sits for a moment
on your wrist: this therapy won't stop death. 'The data doesn't
support that conclusion, Susan. Merely that it helps lessen risk.'

The fact slowly opens and closes its wings.

Note: genes can be turned on and off by circumstances and drugs.
'Adjuvant' means to help in advance (trying to prevent recurrence or
spread). In Ovid's Metamorphosis, threatened people change. Papilionoidea
are butterflies.

Wee Sleekit Cowrin' Beastie

Hello, I'm your melanoma. Think of me as a mouse, nesting
in the first cosy place I came to, between trouser leg and sock.

Good for catching rays on a summer's afternoon, magnified
if possible by loch water, sea, a boat or windsurf deck.

I like the way you rub me with cotton on warm days,
wool in the winter. Nurture my little brownish curling back.

Not as cute as field mice asleep in buttercups or flax,
but I'm as sly as the wood mouse in your shed, sashaying

out to feed in broad daylight on seed you left, without
you knowing I am growing by the minute. Changing shape.

What if you'd realized sooner? Recognised my face, paw-prints,
as their verminous invasive selves. Had me taken out.

Note: melanoma is a highly dangerous, rapidly spreading skin cancer, thought to be caused by UV exposure. It is essential to act promptly to have your skin checked if any pigmentation changes.

Change into this please

This one opens / closes at the back.
This one opens / closes at the front.
This one wraps around,
but you can leave it open.
This one covers your arse,
but you can leave your knickers on.

You can put this on in a moment,
if you like. Wouldn't you like? But,
'Why are you sitting there naked?'
nobody says.
'Please get undressed, but
not so that you are naked,'
nobody says.

You will have a full skin exam, once a year.
Surely you will need to get undressed,
so that you are naked.
No need for, 'Anything under here?'
which is an ocean
more embarrassing
than revealing the jetsam of your pubic hair.

What if you could magically change
into a plastic mannikin
just for consultations,
so they could all do
whatever they like to you
and nobody would care?

Banana Circus

Bananas in spangled coconut bras.
Bananas on horseback on tips of tails,
skins peeled and flipped into striped layer skirts.
Bananas with teaspoons in skinny hands
teeter across a high wire, balancing.
Bananas boom out of a shiny canon.
One banana faking it, with a knife
stuck through the middle of his fleshy parts.
Somehow, all the bananas are grinning.
All this documented in black and white.

You spent childhood time with these bananas.
You didn't believe then such things could
be possible, reading the big red book
on your grandparents' attic floor. But now
you want to believe in impossibles.
Slip on a pair of red tails and top hat,
a curly moustache. Be a banana,
if it would help. Become a banana
ringmaster, cracking your whip to dismiss
big cats, anything with an appetite.

What they don't tell you about surgery

You really do feel as if you are on a table.
You can hear them laying out the cutlery.
You can't say: may I get down now, please?
Or pass the salt, or this lasagna is delicious.
You are to be a mere carpaccio of yourself.

Nobody will notice when you cry, if the area
in question/for attention is at the other end.
Nobody says grace. You are a hostage guest.
They lay the tablecloth on top of your body.
The object is to get what's eating you, out.

At least they don't sharpen the knives
in front of you, before the carving starts.
If it's general anaesthetic that you prefer,
there'll be a genial sommelier, with patter
ready about feeling like you've had a few,

cherry blossom and blue sky in a square
of halogen above you, or a green wall frieze
of flowers from a Swiss taverna to admire
as they pump in sedative, pre-ketamine.
A gentleman raises his courteous, large hand,

then clamps a gas cup on your face. Punch-
drunk you struggle and the moment before
you do succumb, you realise you will disappear
from yourself on a table in a room set for lunch,
full of strangers ready to get stuck in. Too late.

Drains

BBC Wildlife Instagram shows
a snake (green)
stretching its fangs (white)
like actual pearly teeth -
no holes visible
except for its
mouth,
like the opening of a drain
but beautifully patterned,
rhomboid
like medical dressing
mesh.

Drains inserted during surgery
into your leg,
are not like anything.
Do not seem well enough
attached.
No teeth keep them in place.
A piece of tape
(opaque).
Tubing

(yellow, red).
Removing elements of you &
sliding down your thigh
in unhuman
parabola.

Nowhere near
as safe
as a snake in bed.

Only remove
when running clear.

Mr Rex and I

Surgeon has a mug with a dinosaur whose tiny arms
add punch to the red joke line,
'If you're happy and you know it, clap your hands'.

The assumption is: everything is ok. Surgeon looks fit,
trail-running shoes under pinstripe trews.
Thick cotton sleeves, always rolled up to the elbows.

Nothing wrong with his professional claws.
And always grimly grinning, whatever the news. 'Very good
to see you again.'

Clapping is not part of today's performance.
I am on pause.

Wild Type

Wild child. Wild woman. Wild bird. Wild beast.
Wild Thing. Wild times. Wild place. Wilderness.

I want to be wild and as God intended.
I want to be wild and free from my genes'
mutations. But I am not 'Wild Type', according to Doc,
I am BRAF. Melanoma is in me. I am a gene mutant.

Don't panic, these days we can turn it off. After
a few rounds of choppity-chop, pop back for a slice more
or two perhaps, a nice, neat graft and medallion of pork

(we can do that these days, pig meat into persons
in one outpatient slot). Leave you looking attacked
by a small square shark, nothing worse.

Add seaweed and silver
to wounds that won't heal and if need be, open
your thigh, the back of your knee, un-staple your groin,

perform a complete dissection of lymph nodes
sieving rogue cancer on the move from your original
Apollo's ankle attack.

Then once you're clear, like pruning the garden in November,
ready for over winter, we'll see what we can do about that gene
which got turned on at the prospect of you,

in all your available fleshy glory. Waiting to spring
more surprises, under the beds of your lungs
or hidden in the duvet of your brain.

You're lucky.
Gene therapy's come on so much recently. This
chemo for a year will reduce the risk of recurrence
by fifteen percent. Tips you over 50/50. A pretty
good bet, I'd say. And yes, Doncaster Wildlife Park
is a decent day out. Do remember to wear a hat.

Note: 'BRAF' gene mutations make certain treatments possible, although they also make melanoma more likely to occur. Without that mutation, you are 'Wild Type'. Apollo is god of the sun, illness and healing, poetry and prophecy.

Hot Woman

I'm hot.
You're hot.
He, she, or it is hot.

Everybody knows how to conjugate hot.

Open a window. Stand in a fridge. Take your clothes off.

Everyone knows how to solve the problem.

They sure do
tell you
often enough.

But what is this blooming rabid pink,
increasing to acid molten red now
heat you've got evolving, yet again?

You can't unboil this egg, turn off this kettle. Say, 'Ta-ta, volcano.'

A seamount vent arises
inside your chest, whilst
the water of your living room

normality masks
a subterranean force, this chemical
molecular reactor, between your breasts.

Gradually, you discover, physical activity is the spark.

You must be the hottest woman in the country,
just picking up a cup,
cutting a slice of bread, or throwing a toy for a dog.

There should be a calendar of you:

Hot Woman

in the kitchen,
in the garden,
back in bed.

Mrs Sisyphus

Man on chemo cycles 1,000 miles and
you walked back from the chemist
for the first time,
tipping your hat to yourself and the flowers,
rolling the balled stone of your body
all the way up our long road's hill,
only to find at the last
an email from your mother:
man on chemo cycles 1,000 miles.

sharks don't get cancer.

Feel your spots
in the swimming pool,
pausing to wallow
at the shallow end -
a bit of jelly left to swill

around the bowl
of the wide medium lane,
at Heeley City Baths, 2.15.
Mayfly-legged people all
come circle round again.

Double up, reach
down, and grunting
(un-heard between us
all slip-slapping away),
stretch back to the sucker

setting up camp, on a soft
white beach-bend, behind
the outcrop of your knee,
where the lymph
-nodes used to be.

Remove your goggles.
Hold your lung-full for a spell.
Hang still in neutral buoyancy.
Then remember, sharks cannot
do that. But, then again,

Note: this is a circular poem, continuing from the end back through the title. Sadly, gene therapy does not guarantee cancer recurrence won't happen, nor that it won't metastasise (spread to other organs – known as Stage 4 cancer). Sharks, however, according to biologists, are remarkable because they do not appear to suffer from cancer at all.

Hope Is A Thing With Cells
(after Emily Dickinson, in praise of immunotherapy)

It's 8.15 in the morning and I'm googling -
Chinese Hamster Taxidermy -
because buying the animal
whose ovaries have grown
my biologic treatment - and doing life drawings of it -
is going to save me.

This is hope - the shape it comes in - this morning.

Mouse Taxidermy Holiday Rodent. Taxidermy Mouse in Bathtub. Real Mouse in Bathtub Fun. End of Days Taxidermy Mouse - all available for real - *Sacrificed Mouse Taxidermy + Taxidermy Mouse Plans of World Domination.*

Great prices. Fast delivery.

I can buy my way out of cancer, on Etsy, with style.
Bid my way, on Ebay, out of bad directions my forking life might take.
Bungle some kind of bogus altar together - to keep me safe - while I wait

for the bazaar of modern science to change my immune system's cells.

Wet Specimen Chinese Dwarf Hamster
offered for sale, turns out had a tumour.
Not that one then - or stuff it myself - put it out
for the garden death gods: please eat her, save me?
Back to Pinterest. Next. *Taxidermy Dwarf Hamster*
by Precious Creature: *cute necklace*. Just yuk.

A-taxidermist-is-the-keeper-of-a-quiet-zoo. Yeah, very quiet.

I could be a noiseless patient, if I'm not careful, but what can you do?
I can't control what's stuffing me. My Chinese Hamster ovary proteins
are now romping - on the loose - silently replacing Programmed Death Cell 1.
     I hope.

Note: immunotherapy has greatly improved many cancer treatment outcomes, especially for Stage 4 melanoma, for which traditional chemotherapy is not very effective. The drugs are made from the Chinese Hamster species. However, the long-term results are, as yet, unclear. Apollo, god of the sun, illness and healing, is said to have sometimes appeared in mouse form.

The Coffin Road

We walked over the coffin road
once in the Lakes and the rain.

                    It was when I still had all of me.
                    Of both legs, inner thighs and groin.

We slipped up coursing flags.
Marveled at ancient casket-men,

                    I imagine now shouldering
                    tiny, boxed parts of myself,

with equal gravity, negotiating
vertiginous bracken streams.

                    Lymph nodes and tissue dissected
                    from the left bank, where my legs join.

It never occurred to me to ask you:
Why was there no church this side?

                    What happened to those pieces
                    once they'd given up their secrets?

One valley consecrated, split
by a ridge from the next, un-tithed?

                    Nobody buried my bits of flesh.
                    Incineration is standard for cancer.

We ate apples under a tree, backs
to hawthorn hedges, wet to the skin

                    though wearing clothes, I might as well
                    have been naked, for all the good.

Note: 'coffin roads' are old rural routes used to carry coffins from an area without a church to the nearest consecrated burial ground. In The Lakes, some go over tricky hillsides.

On cutting my hair before Stereotactic Radiosurgery on my brain

Is the sun an event or a place?
Is it a cosmic something always becoming or
continuously disintegrating outwards,
in filaments of light
and heat and energy and all those things that physicists like?

This is what goes on inside my head,
while I cut my hair a week before my brain
is to be subjected to
Stereotactic Radiosurgery –
Gamma Knife – in a titanium cage, to be screwed into my skull.

Is my metastasis an event or a place?
Is it absorbing, eating, using the energy of the universe,
continuously seeding
its cell-increasing-self –
a deadly remnant of the Big Bang playing out? I mean, where else

can this growth's energy have once begun?
There are no other batteries, power plants, cosmic origins.
I plug my clippers in.
The met lurks within.
After this round, I'll let my head fight back. Become the sun.

I will grow my hair into more than a halo.
I will grow my hair in a corona of solar flares.
I will charge myself up like a Van de Graaff generator, then stare
my melanoma metastases down,
with a mane of blond static shock.

If the sun is a place,
if my metastases are a place,
they are about to find out where the line is drawn.
Straight out of my head, again and again and again.
If they are an event, well, all things come to an end.

Note: Stereotactic Radiosurgery treats brain metastases via multiple beams aimed at the cancer, whilst the patient's head is kept still by a cage screwed into their skull and locked down. It has a very high success rate. It was originally called Gamma Knife but isn't often referred to that way these days for patients.

The Truth About Hats

In Sparta, there's a helmet
with a hole in it.
Genuine spear gash
you can see right through.

So much more effective
for conveying the truth
about hats
than any old fedora in the hall.

Charm

Some mornings you are satisfied with yellow.
Daylight on the cold frame frost-house door.
Daffodils, so long in coming on, now out-stay
their welcome against nasturtiums, spread
the garden with rills of cool yellow butter.
If you were to light your back yard cube
as a stage, Sicilian dusty lunchtime Lemon
Daylight would be good. Pick out the apple
blossom with a tint of Timeless Sunshine.
Everything would be so satisfactory.
Yellow against the sky-blue half of the fence
you painted, post-op bank holiday, last year.
Pale sheet petals wait, sleepy, slightly listing.
As you write this line, two goldfinches arrive.

Note: 'charm' is the collective noun for goldfinches
and also refers to an object to ward off illness or ill will.

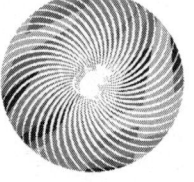

ACKNOWLEDGEMENTS

Thank you to the all the staff at Weston Park Hospital and Royal Hallamshire Hospital, Sheffield, who have kept and still keep me alive, including the Skin Cancer Specialist Nurse Team, especially Charlotte Wain, Janette Phillips and Mandy Parkin; the consultants, Mr AJ Stephenson, Dr Shobna Silva, Dr James Maxwell, Dr Miguel Debono, Dr Jo Bird (who has often cheered me up) and most of all, Dr Krishna Garadi; the Stereotactic Radiosurgery team (who have listened to me recite poetry whilst injecting my head) and umpteen radiographers; all the wonderful so-called Junior Doctors; the Immunotherapy treatment team (including for all the great reading recommendations); all the other nurses and phlebotomists; every kind receptionist; and Steven Brown, who is better at physio than topiary. A special thank you to Dr Kerry Ware, for helping me learn how to live with less suffering.

Thank you to my family (especially my wife and my mother) and friends who have supported me throughout both treatment and writing. Mack, thank you for all the love and care which you've never stopped giving. Lucy, thank you for ringing. Special thanks for wonderful supportive friendship to Jules Rushforth, Angela Neenan, Jean Reid, Kathy Coyne and Alice Willington.

Thank you poetry friends: Kitty Donnelly (especially for giving my melanoma poems a first home), Peter Clarke, Katie Jukes, Katherine Moss, peers and tutors at Manchester Metropolitan University's Writing School, Sheffield Central Library poetry people all for lending your ears, the Mid-Derby Poetry Stanza and Liz Coatman for giving this whole thing a great editorial kicking. Thank you also to Peter and Ann Sansom for their early encouragement and feedback on some of these poems.

Huge thanks to Jamie Hale and Pascale Petit for choosing this pamphlet for the Disabled Poets Prize and for all their generous advice, support and friendship since. Thank you also to Ruth Harrison of Spread the Word for everything she does to make the prize possible.

ABOUT THE AUTHOR

Half poet, half tutor, half clown and Winner of the Disabled Poets Prize 2024, **Susie Wilson** has worn many hats. A former prop maker, theatre manager, lawyer and English teacher, she now tutors, draws and plays jazz piano (though not at the same time). She is a Scottish auDHD writer currently living in Sheffield with two beardy dogs, her wife, a diagnosis of advanced melanoma (hats are now essential) and the intention of training in clowning while continuing to write as long as she can.

Susie has poems out now in *Propel, Ink Sweat & Tears, Northern Gravy, Black Bough* and *Envoi*, forthcoming in *Carmen et Error*. Her poetry has previously been widely published in anthologies and has been commended and listed including by *Poets & Players* and *The Rialto* Nature competitions. Her work also includes collaboration with composers at the Royal Northern College of Music and a commission from the Sheffield Philharmonic Chorus. A micro-chapbook, *Skin The Rabbit*, about growing up in Scotland, on the outside looking in, will be out with *The Braag* in Spring 2025.

Her work explores time, vulnerability and the absurdity of life and nature. Follow Susie on @concordmoose.bsky.social or www.susiewilsonpoet.com

FURTHER READING for anyone concerned about Melanoma:

www.melanomafocus.org
www.cancerresearchuk.org/about-cancer/melanoma

Including skin changes to look out for:
www.britishskinfoundation.org.uk/what-is-skin-cancer

Fortunately Melanoma treatment has advanced greatly and is continuously improving, thus the statistics referred to in some poems will be even better now.

ABOUT VERVE POETRY PRESS

Verve Poetry Press is an award-winning press which focussed initially on meeting a local need in Birmingham - a need for the vibrant poetry scene here in Brum to find a way to present itself to the poetry world via publication. Co-founded by Stuart Bartholomew and Amerah Saleh, it now publishes poets from all corners of the UK and beyond - poets that speak to the city's varied and energetic qualities and will contribute to its many poetic stories.

Added to this is a colourful pamphlet series, many featuring poets who have performed at our sister festival - and a poetry show series which captures the magic of longer poetry performance pieces by festival alumni such as Polarbear, Kevin P. Gilday and Imogen Stirling.

The press has been voted Most Innovative Publisher at the Saboteur Awards, and has won the Publisher's Award for Poetry Pamphlets at the Michael Marks Awards.

Like the festival, we strive to think about poetry in inclusive ways and embrace the multiplicity of approaches towards this glorious art.

https://vervepoetrypress.com
@VervePoetryPres
mail@vervepoetrypress.com